# The Magic School Bus®

## A science FACT FINDER

# SPACE
## and the
# PLANETS

**SCHOLASTIC INC.**

New York   Toronto   London   Auckland   Sydney
Mexico City   New Delhi   Hong Kong   Buenos Aires

Written by Kris Hirschmann.

Cover illustrations by Peter Bollinger and Carolyn Bracken.
Interior illustrations by Carisa Swenson, Ted Enik, and Carolyn Bracken.

Based on *The Magic School Bus* books
written by Joanna Cole and illustrated by Bruce Degen.

This book is a nonfiction companion
to *The Magic School Bus: Space Explorers.*

The author would like to thank Gregory Vogt of Colorado State University
for his expert advice in reviewing this manuscript.

ISBN 0-439-38175-4

12  11  10  9  8  7  6  5  4                              3/0 4/0 5/0 6/0

Cover design by Carisa Swenson
Interior designed by Madalina Stefan

Printed in the U.S.A.                                    40

First Scholastic printing, October 2002

Visit Scholastic.com for information about our books and authors online!

# Contents

A Note from Ms. Frizzle     iv

**Chapter 1**

The Solar System     1

**Chapter 2**

The Sun     10

**Chapter 3**

The Inner Planets     16

**Chapter 4**

The Gas Giants     28

**Chapter 5**

On the Fringes     40

**Chapter 6**

Asteroids, Meteoroids, and Comets     45

**Chapter 7**

Beyond the Solar System     53

**Chapter 8**

Exploring Space     60

**Chapter 9**

Space Myths     70

Index     81

# A Note from Ms. Frizzle

Dear Readers,

Before my class boards the Magic School Bus, I always do my research. I find out as much as I can about where we are going and what we will learn there. With a little digging, I always discover a treasure trove of fascinating facts.

When we became Space Explorers, I came ready with all the facts I could find about space and the solar system. By the end of the trip, my students were real space experts, too. You could say it was far-out!

We are excited to share all we have learned from our space unit. You can use the facts you read about here in a report of your own.

Good luck,
Ms. Frizzle

# The Magic School Bus®

## A Science FACT FINDER

# SPACE
## and the
# PLANETS

OUR SOLAR SYSTEM *

PLUTO

NEPTUNE

URANUS

SATURN

JUPITER

MARS

VENUS

SUN

MERCURY

THE MOON

ASTEROID BELT

EARTH

* The word SOLAR comes from the Latin word SOL, which means SUN.

This chapter is out of this world!

# Chapter 1
## The Solar System

For thousands of years, people thought Earth was the center of the universe. Today, we know this is not true. Earth is important to us because it is our home. But in the "big picture," Earth is just one tiny body moving through the unimaginably large expanse of outer space.

Earth is not alone on its journey. It is part of a neighborhood of bodies that includes the sun, the moon, comets, asteroids, other planets, and more. This neighborhood is called the solar system.

## What Is the Solar System?

The solar system is made up of the sun and all the objects that *orbit* (revolve around) it. The main orbiting bodies are the nine known planets: Mercury, Venus, Earth, Mars, Jupiter, Saturn, Uranus, Neptune, and Pluto. Six of these planets have orbiting objects of their own, called moons. There are 91 known moons in the solar system, and there are probably many more still to be discovered.

Scientists have discovered 30 new moons since 1998. Twelve of these moons orbit Jupiter, 12 orbit Saturn, and six orbit Uranus.

In addition to the planets and their moons, there are many other objects orbiting the sun, including asteroids, meteoroids, comets, and gigantic clouds of dust and gas.

The solar system is enormous. Pluto, the outermost planet, is sometimes as much as 4.5 billion miles (7.3 billion km) from the sun. But the solar system extends much farther than that.

Scientists believe that the most distant edges of the solar system may be 11 billion miles (17.6 billion km) from the sun.

### Circling and Spinning

A planet rotates around an imaginary line running through the middle of the planet, from top to bottom, called an *axis*. Each planet's axis is tilted at a different angle.

The nine planets and their moons orbit the sun, all in the same direction. Seven of the planets orbit on roughly the same plane, which means that their paths can all be traced on the same flat surface. Mercury and Pluto are different from the rest of the planets. Their orbits are tilted away from the plane the others occupy.

Orbits are not perfect circles. They are shaped more like ovals. Because of this, a planet's distance from the sun is not constant. At some times a planet is closer to the sun, and at other times it is farther away.

## Changing Seasons

The tilt of Earth's axis creates our seasons. The axis is always tilted at the same angle. As a result, different regions of Earth are tilted toward the sun depending on where Earth is in its orbit. When a region is tilted toward the sun, it is summertime in that area. When the same region is tilted away from the sun, it is wintertime.

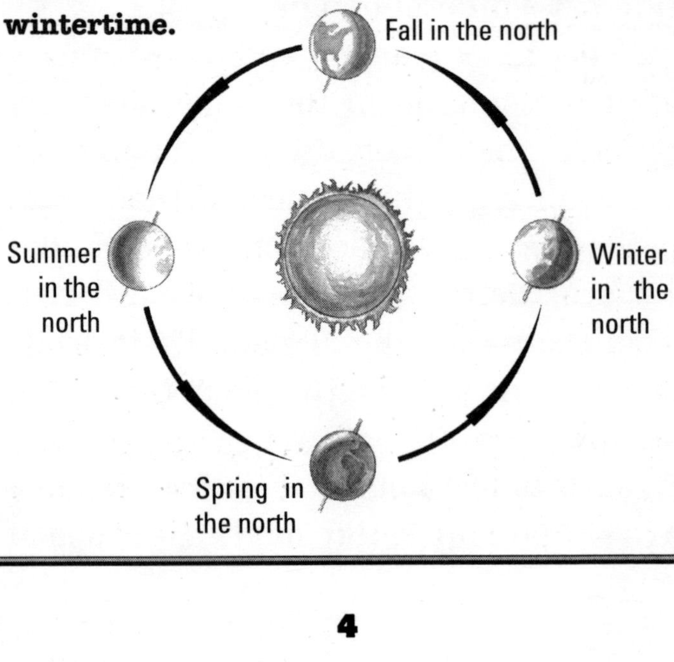

Fall in the north

Summer in the north

Winter in the north

Spring in the north

One full orbit is called a year. Planets closest to the sun travel faster, so it takes them less time to complete an orbit. That means the planets closest to the sun have shorter years than the planets farthest away. Mercury's year, for example, is only 88 Earth days long. But faraway Pluto takes more than 248 Earth years to complete one orbit!

## Speeding Through Space

The closer a planet is to the sun, the faster it travels. Mercury, the innermost planet, zooms around the sun at a speedy 30 miles per second (48 kps). Pluto, the farthest planet from the sun, is the slowpoke of the solar system. It only goes about 3 miles per second (4.8 kps).

Earth travels at about 18.6 miles per second (30 kps).

As planets orbit the sun, they *rotate*, or spin around and around. This rotation causes day and night. When your side of Earth is facing the sun, it's daytime where you live. When your side is facing away from the sun, day turns to night. One full spin, or rotation, is called a day. The length of a day changes from planet to planet. A day on Jupiter is less than 10 Earth hours long, while Venus's day is more than 117 Earth days long!

## Birth of the Solar System

Scientists believe that the solar system started out as a huge cloud of dust and gas. About five billion years ago this cloud began to collapse inward. The center of the cloud became thicker and hotter until eventually the sun was born.

Right away other bodies began to form in the cooler outer parts of the cloud. Bits of dust collided. Gravity made them stick together, and they formed small clumps. These clumps collided to become larger clumps, then even larger, and so on. Within about 10 million years, most of the dust had become the rocky inner planets, Mercury, Venus, Earth, and Mars. Farther out, the gas in the original dust cloud

*Gravitation* is a force of attraction that exists between all objects. The more massive an object, the more gravitation it exerts. Earth exerts a gravitational force, too. That's what keeps your feet on the ground and keeps you from flying into space.

The sun is the largest object in the solar system. Its gravitational pull is strong enough to keep the planets, comets, asteroids, and other bodies in their places. Without gravity, everything in the solar system would drift off into outer space!

formed the giant planets, Jupiter, Saturn, Uranus, and Neptune. Leftover dust, gas, and ice became the moons, asteroids, comets, and other bodies still present in today's solar system.

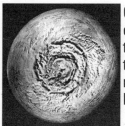

Clumps of dust stuck together to form rocky Mars.

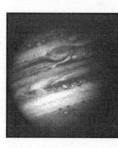

Jupiter is full of gas from the dust cloud that formed the solar system.

7

**The Solar System Today and Tomorrow**

Objects still collide in the solar system. But collisions don't happen as often as they used to. This is partly because most of the rocky matter in the solar system has been "used up"

If you built a scale model of the solar system in which the sun was the size of a bowling ball, the edges of the solar system would have to be over a mile away!

by the planets and moons. Another reason is that the solar system is more stable than it used to be. Most objects

## Cosmic Craters

When a large body hits a planet or a moon, it leaves a circular dent called an *impact crater*. On Earth, weather and geological activity wear these dents away over time. But some planets are considered "dead" bodies. They have no atmosphere, or gases, surrounding them. They also have no volcanoes or earthquakes that might change the planet's surface. On "dead" planets, impact craters never disappear.

move along predictable paths, reducing the chance of random collisions.

Earth's moon is covered with impact craters. Most of these craters are billions of years old.

Still, the solar system is not done changing. Collisions will keep happening, and some of them will be major. Also, the sun will eventually get so hot that it will expand and engulf many planets, including Earth. Luckily for us, this won't happen for another 4.5 to 5 billion years or so — about 70 million times longer than the average human life span.

In July 1994, several comet fragments slammed into Jupiter. A comet is an orbiting ball of icy dust and gas. The impact created explosions that rose more than 1,875 miles (3,000 km) high.

# Chapter 2

## The Sun

The sun sits at the center of our solar system. This huge body produces the heat and light energy that make life possible on Earth. It also holds the solar system together through its gravitational pull.

The sun is a star. To us, the sun looks much larger and brighter than any other star. But that's only because it is so close to us. The sun is about 93 million

You could fit more than a million Earths inside the sun.

miles (150 million km) from Earth. Our next closest star, Proxima Centauri, is about 265,000 times more distant!

It takes about eight minutes for light to travel from the sun to Earth. It takes more than four *years* for light to travel from Proxima Centauri to Earth!

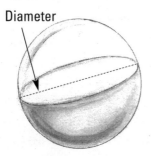
Diameter

*Diameter* is the distance straight through the center of a circle.

### Sun Stats

Like all stars, the sun is a fiery ball of gas. Its diameter is an enormous 865,000 miles (1,392,000 km) — about 110 times the diameter of Earth. The sun is also incredibly massive. It weighs a thousand times more than everything else in the solar system combined!

The sun's power comes from its center, which is called the core. In the core, intense heat and pressure force hydrogen

The sun gives off about 40 percent of its energy as light. The other 60 percent is heat. The sun's light and heat energy stream outward through space at a speed of 186,000 miles per second (297,600 kps). Earth receives only one two-billionth of all the energy the sun gives out!

Tiny particles called *protons* and *neutrons* also stream from the sun. These streaming particles are called the *solar winds*, and they blow throughout the solar system.

atoms to join together. This process is called *nuclear fusion*, and it creates vast amounts of energy. The energy comes out of the core in all directions as light and heat. It travels through several inner layers before reaching the sun's outer layer, which is called the *photosphere*. The photosphere is the part of the sun that we see.

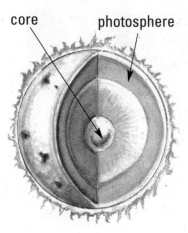

core    photosphere

The photosphere is not a very pleasant place. It is a heaving, bubbling lake of fire with a temperature around 10,000 degrees Fahrenheit (5,540 degrees Celsius). But that's downright cool compared to the core, where temperatures reach 27 million degrees Fahrenheit (15 million degrees Celsius). Now *that's* hot!

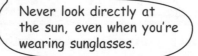

Never look directly at the sun, even when you're wearing sunglasses.

Huge tongues of flame sometimes erupt from the sun's surface. These tongues are called *solar flares*.

## The Sun's Life Cycle

The sun will not always look the way it does today. Several billion years from now the sun will have used up most of the hydrogen "fuel" in its core. At that point the sun will start to expand, growing into a type of star called a red giant. During this period the sun will get so large that it will eat up the inner planets!

### Total Eclipse of the Sun

Sometimes the moon passes directly between the sun and Earth. When this happens, the moon casts a shadow on Earth. To a person standing in the shadow, it looks like the sun is covered by a dark disk. This is called a total eclipse of the sun.

A total eclipse lasts only a few minutes. During this time, the sun's ghostly *corona* (gaseous atmosphere) can be seen. We can't see the corona at other times because the sun's photosphere shines too brightly.

Remember, *never* look directly at the sun, *especially* during an eclipse. The bright light could permanently damage your eyes!

Solar eclipse

After the red giant phase, the sun will begin to shrink. When it is done shrinking, the sun will be smaller and cooler than it is today. It will be a weak white dwarf, and the solar system will be a much colder and darker place.

The sun contains 99.8 percent of the matter in the solar system.

Let's take a closer look at our nearest neighbors.

# Chapter 3
## The Inner Planets

The four planets closest to the sun — Mercury, Venus, Earth, and Mars — are small and rocky. As a group, they are sometimes called the terrestrial planets. (Terrestrial means "earthlike.")

### Mercury

Mercury is the innermost planet in the solar system. Because it is so close to the sun, Mercury gets incredibly hot. Daytime temperatures rise above 700 degrees Fahrenheit (370 degrees Celsius)!

At night, however, all that heat escapes and the temperature plunges. During the dark hours, temperatures on Mercury drop to –275 degrees Fahrenheit (–170 degrees Celsius).

One Mercury day is equal to almost six Earth months. This long day is part of the

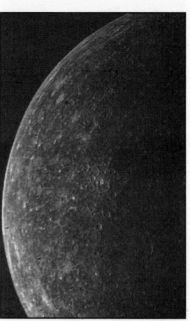

Hot Mercury has some ice! The ice is hidden inside deep polar craters.

reason for Mercury's extreme temperatures. The sun shines on the same part of the planet for weeks at a time — long enough to get things really hot. Night lasts for weeks, too, giving Mercury's blistering surface plenty of time to cool down.

Mercury is crisscrossed by tall, rocky

cliffs. It is also covered with craters, most of which are billions of years old. Mercury has no atmosphere, so there is nothing to wear these features down.

### Venus

Venus is the second planet from the sun.

Because it is almost the same size as Earth, Venus is sometimes called our "sister planet."

Venus rotates in the opposite direction from all the other planets in the solar system.

Conditions on Venus are much more extreme than on Earth. For starters, the entire planet is blanketed by thick yellow clouds of sulfuric acid. Scientists believe that these clouds sometimes rain acid onto Venus's surface. The surface itself has some active volcanoes that belch hot lava and deadly fumes. The planet's atmosphere consists mostly of

## The Star That Isn't a Star

After the moon, Venus is the brightest object in Earth's night sky. Venus can only be seen during a few months each year, and it only appears for a couple of hours before dawn or after dusk. Because of this timing, Venus is sometimes called the morning star or the evening star. But it's not a star. It's a planet! It doesn't give off any light of its own. Instead, it reflects the light of the sun — just as our moon does.

poisonous carbon dioxide gas. And the air pressure at ground level is high enough to crush a person!

As if these features weren't bad enough, Venus is also the hottest planet in the solar system. Venus's clouds and atmosphere trap the energy of the sun's rays and keep it from escaping into space. This phenomenon is called the *greenhouse effect*. Because of the greenhouse effect, Venus's temperature can rise to 900 degrees Fahrenheit (480 degrees Celsius). That's more than four times as hot as boiling water!

Although several probes have landed

### Things Are Really Heating Up

Earth has its own greenhouse effect, thanks to the gases in the atmosphere. In the last few centuries, the atmosphere has become polluted, and is trapping more heat than ever before. This is heating up Earth's climate, an effect scientists call *global warming*.

on Venus, none lasted more than a couple of hours. Venus's heat and pressure destroyed them all. But orbiting spacecraft have had better luck. Using radar, these vehicles have been able to map most of Venus's surface.

### Earth

Earth is the third planet from the sun. Seen from space, our home planet is a swirl of different colors. White clouds,

Earth is the only planet in the solar system with oceans of liquid water.

Earth has one natural *satellite* (orbiting body). Our satellite is our moon, and it is the brightest object in our night sky. The brightness we see is the sun's light reflecting off the moon's dark surface.

At any time, half of the moon's surface is lit by the sun. But we don't always see the lit side. We see different amounts of light depending on where the moon is in its orbit. That's why the moon seems to *wax* (get bigger) and *wane* (get smaller) during its 27-day journey around Earth.

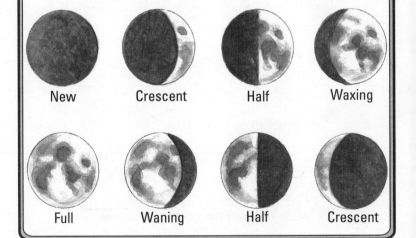

New     Crescent     Half     Waxing

Full     Waning     Half     Crescent

brown soil, and green vegetation can be seen. But because about 70 percent of Earth is covered with water, the main color is a beautiful deep blue.

Earth's watery surface is unique in the solar system. On hotter planets, water is a vapor. On colder planets, it freezes into ice. But on Earth, the temperature is just right. We are at exactly the right distance from the sun for oceans to exist.

Thanks to its perfect distance from the sun, our planet has another unique quality. It is the only planet in the solar system that supports life. All living things need water, so liquid water is a big

Until a few hundred years ago, people thought the sun orbited Earth.

part of the reason for life on Earth. Earth's atmosphere is also important. Not only does our atmosphere give us the oxygen we need to breathe, it also regulates Earth's temperature and blocks most of the sun's harmful rays. If Earth were just a few million miles closer to or farther from the sun, conditions would be too harsh for life.

There could be other planets in other solar systems that support life. But if life exists elsewhere, humans haven't discovered it yet. So far, Earth is the only place in the universe where life is known to exist.

## Mars

Mars is the fourth planet from the sun. Most of Mars is covered with rusty sand and rocks that give the planet a red tint.

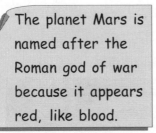
The planet Mars is named after the Roman god of war because it appears red, like blood.

In some ways, Mars is similar to Earth. It has polar ice caps, just like Earth does. It also has dried-up riverbeds and lake basins, which means that Mars had liquid water sometime in the past. The planet has deep canyons, sandy deserts, and extinct volcanoes.

## Mountains of Mars

One of the extinct volcanoes on Mars, Olympus Mons, is the largest volcano in the solar system. The base of Olympus Mons is as big as the state of Arizona. The volcano's peak rises almost three times higher than Mount Everest, Earth's tallest mountain!

Mars's weather is also similar to Earth's in some ways. Mars has four seasons, just like Earth. Its day is about the same length as ours, and surface temperatures sometimes rise above 75 degrees Fahrenheit (24 degrees Celsius) — a comfortable temperature for humans.

Mars is sometimes called the Red Planet.

Because of all these similarities, scientists thought for a long time that life might exist on Mars. But many space probes have explored Mars, and none has found any evidence of life. They discovered instead that Mars is mostly a rocky desert with a thin, unbreathable atmosphere. Although daytime temperatures can be moderate, Mars's temperature plunges as low as −193 degrees Fahrenheit (−125 degrees Celsius) at night. The planet experiences huge, violent windstorms that can kick up enough dust to fill the skies. It is also the home of giant tornadoes called dust devils. With these harsh conditions, life probably could not exist on Mars.

**Mercury Facts**

Year:         88 Earth days

Day:          176 Earth days

Diameter:     3,032 miles (4,879 km)

Moons:        None

Average distance from sun: 36 million miles (58 million km)

## Venus Facts

Year:       225 Earth days
Day:        117 Earth days
Diameter:   12,104 miles (19,366 km)
Moons:      None
Average distance from sun: 67 million miles (108 million km)

## Earth Facts

Year:       365 Earth days
Day:        24 hours
Diameter:   12,756 miles (20,530 km)
Moons:      1
Average distance from sun: 93 million miles (150 million km)

## Mars Facts

Year:       687 Earth days
Day:        24.7 hours
Diameter:   4,222 miles (6,794 km)
Moons:      2
Average distance from sun: 143 million miles (228 million km)

> If you think Earth is big, check out these giant balls of gas!

# Chapter 4
## The Gas Giants

You have read that the first four planets of the solar system are small and rocky. The next four planets — Jupiter, Saturn, Uranus, and Neptune — are very different. They are huge, and their outer layers are made of gas. So these planets are sometimes called the *gas giants*.

### Jupiter

Jupiter is the fifth planet from the sun, and it is by far the biggest and heaviest planet in the solar system.

Jupiter is so big that you could fit almost 1,300 Earths inside it.

Jupiter is twice as heavy as the rest of the planets combined!

Jupiter probably has a small rocky core a few times larger than Earth. The rest of this gigantic planet is mostly hydrogen gas. Near the core, incredible pressure squeezes the hydrogen into a metal. Farther out, the hydrogen becomes a liquid, and farther still, a gas. The gas layer is about 625 miles (1,000 km) deep, and it forms Jupiter's surface.

Despite its enormous size, Jupiter spins very fast. It makes one rotation in less than 10 hours! This speedy spinning separates Jupiter's gassy clouds into multicolored bands. It also creates some very violent weather. A recent probe measured wind speeds of 450 miles per hour (720 kph) within Jupiter's atmosphere. That's six times faster than hurricane winds blow on Earth!

Jupiter's dark bands are called *belts*. The light bands are called *zones*.

Jupiter's most famous feature, the Great Red Spot, is a hurricanelike storm

## I Coulda Been a Star!

The planet Jupiter is built a lot like the sun. Scientists believe that if Jupiter were about 10 times bigger, it would have turned into a star instead of a planet.

Even though it is not a star, Jupiter gives off heat. Its core is hotter than the surface of the sun!

more than three times the size of Earth. This storm was first spotted in the mid-1600s, and it is still raging today. That's some storm!

### Saturn

The sixth planet from the sun, Saturn, is best known for its magnificent ring system. From Earth, Saturn looks like it has three thick rings. But in 1981, a space probe called *Voyager 1* flew close to Saturn and took pictures showing that these thick rings were actually thousands of thin rings.

Saturn is a deep, rich yellow with some faint darker bands.

Saturn's rings are not solid. They are made of millions of orbiting icy rocks. Some of these rocks are as big as houses, and others are as tiny as grains of sand.

This close-up of Saturn's rings shows that they are actually broad bands of thin rings.

Saturn is very similar to Jupiter. It has a small core surrounded by layers of metal, liquid, and gassy hydrogen, plus some other elements. Like Jupiter, Saturn spins very fast, which can cause violent storms. Although Saturn doesn't have any permanent storm systems, it does have shorter storms with wind speeds greater than 1,000 miles per hour

Saturn is not the only planet with rings. The rest of the gas giants have rings, too, although they are much thinner and fainter than the rings of Saturn.

Scientists can "see" rings when a planet passes directly in front of a star. The star blinks a few times before and after the planet passes. Each blink is caused by a ring blocking some of the star's light.

(1,600 kph) — more than twice as fast as Jupiter's!

Of all the planets in the solar system, Saturn has the lowest density. This means that Saturn is not as tightly packed together as the other planets. Saturn is so light for its size that it would float in water — *if* you could find a body of water big enough!

Saturn's fast rotation makes it bulge in the middle. The whole planet looks a little bit squashed.

It is a long journey from Saturn to Uranus, the seventh planet from the sun. Uranus is about twice as far from the sun as Saturn is.

Uranus's strangest feature is its extreme tilt. Uranus's axis of rotation is nearly horizontal, not vertical like the other planets. This means that Uranus is lying on its side as it orbits the sun.

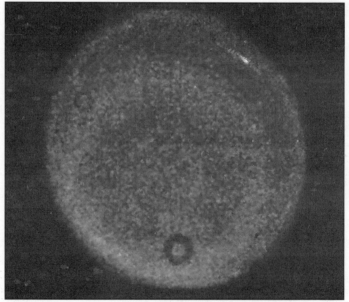

Uranus is much smaller than its neighbors Jupiter and Saturn.

Scientists think that Uranus started out upright like all the other planets. But then an object the size of Earth bumped into Uranus and tipped it over. This collision probably happened billions of years ago, in the early days of the solar system.

Unlike Jupiter and Saturn, Uranus has a core of rock and ice surrounded by thick clouds of water, ammonia, and methane gas. The methane gives Uranus its beautiful blue-green color.

Because of Uranus's weird tilt, every year the planet experiences 42 Earth years of daylight — and then 42 Earth years of darkness.

Uranus was the first planet to be discovered with a telescope.

## Neptune

Neptune is the eighth planet from the sun. It is also the last — and the smallest — of the gas giants. Like Uranus, Neptune is blanketed by clouds of water, ammonia, and methane. The planet is deep blue all over.

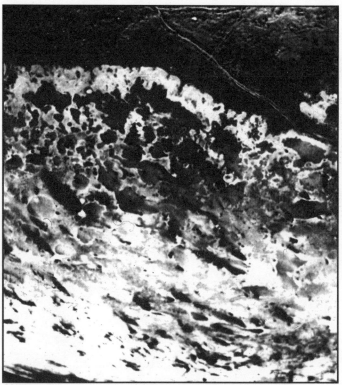

Neptune's atmosphere gives it a deep blue color.

Neptune was discovered by math! In the mid-1800s, scientists realized that Uranus's orbit did not follow its predicted path. They wondered if the gravity of an unknown eighth planet was pulling on Uranus. Mathematical calculations showed them where this eighth planet would be, if indeed it existed. When telescopes were pointed at this location, Neptune was there, right where the equations said it should be.

Other than its location and its size, not much was known about Neptune until 1989, when the space probe *Voyager 2* flew close to the planet. *Voyager 2* discovered that Neptune is the windiest place in the solar system. Huge storms with wind speeds of 1,500 miles per hour (2,400 kph) sometimes blow up within Neptune's gassy atmosphere.

When *Voyager 2* flew by Neptune, it saw a huge storm called the *Great Dark Spot*. This storm was as big as Earth!

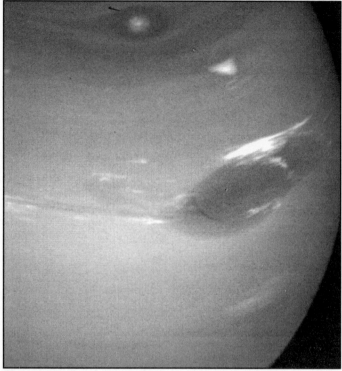

Neptune's Great Dark Spot

**Jupiter Facts**

<u>Year:</u>          11.9 Earth years

<u>Day:</u>          9.9 hours

<u>Diameter:</u>     88,849 miles (142,984 km)

<u>Moons:</u>        28

<u>Average distance from sun:</u> 484 million miles (778 million km)

## Saturn Facts

<u>Year:</u>         29.5 Earth years

<u>Day:</u>          10.7 hours

<u>Diameter:</u>     74,900 miles (120,536 km)

<u>Moons:</u>        30

<u>Average distance from sun:</u> 891 million miles (1.4 billion km)


## Uranus Facts

<u>Year:</u>         84 Earth years

<u>Day:</u>          17.2 hours

<u>Diameter:</u>     31,764 miles (51,118 km)

<u>Moons:</u>        21

<u>Average distance from sun:</u> 1.8 billion miles (2.9 billion km)


## Neptune Facts

<u>Year:</u>         165 Earth years

<u>Day:</u>          16.1 hours

<u>Diameter:</u>     30,776 miles (49,572 km)

<u>Moons:</u>        8

<u>Average distance from sun:</u> 2.8 billion miles (4.5 billion km)

These planets are far-out!

# Chapter 5
## On the Fringes

**B**eyond Neptune, the solar system is mostly a dark, frozen wasteland. It is ringed by a region called the *Kuiper* (KY-per) *Belt* that contains tens of thousands of small, icy bodies. The Kuiper Belt also contains Pluto, the ninth and last planet in the solar system.

### Pluto

Pluto is a tiny, rocky planet. It is the smallest planet in the solar system. Pluto's diameter is less than one-fifth that of Earth!

Pluto is the farthest planet from the sun. It's also the smallest.

Pluto has one moon named Charon (CARE-en). Compared to Pluto, Charon is huge. It is about half the diameter of its mother planet.

Charon does not exactly orbit Pluto. Instead, both bodies circle a point somewhere between the two. For this reason, some scientists say that Pluto

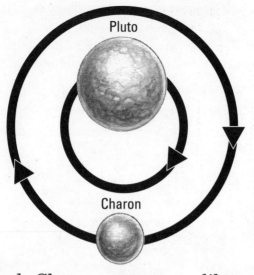

Pluto

Charon

Pluto and Charon both orbit around the same point in space.

and Charon are more like a "double planet" than a planet and a moon.

Other scientists wonder whether Pluto should be called a planet at all. They think it might be more like an asteroid or a comet. But Pluto does have some planetlike features. Like some of the inner planets, it has polar ice caps. And although Pluto has no atmosphere most of the time, it develops a thin layer of methane and nitrogen gases when it is closest to the sun. Finally, Pluto has a spherical shape, like the other planets.

Pluto has the most unusual orbit of any planet. For one thing, Pluto orbits the sun on a different plane, one that is tilted away from the plane on which the other planets orbit. The orbit is also very irregular. At some times, Pluto comes within 2.8 billion miles (4.4 billion km) of the sun. At other times, it is up to 4.7 billion miles (7.5 billion km) away!

Pluto actually travels inside Neptune's orbit for 20 years out of its 248-year orbit. During those 20 years, Neptune is the solar system's outermost planet.

Comets and asteroids are so small that they don't have enough gravity to become spherical. Pluto does. These features have

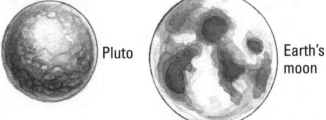

Pluto

Earth's moon

There are seven moons in the solar system that are larger than Pluto. Earth's moon is one of them.

convinced most scientists that Pluto deserves to be called a planet.

## Planet X

Scientists spent decades searching for a tenth planet beyond Pluto. But it now seems unlikely that such a planet exists. Data from space probes suggest that Pluto is the last planet in the solar system. For now, most scientists have stopped looking for the mysterious Planet X.

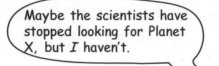

Maybe the scientists have stopped looking for Planet X, but *I* haven't.

### Pluto Facts

Year:      248 Earth years
Day:       6.4 Earth days
Diameter:  1,485 miles (2,390 km)
Moons:     1
Average distance from sun: 3.7 billion miles (5.9 billion km)

Who knew that outer space was filled with so many big rocks?

# Chapter 6
## Asteroids, Meteoroids, and Comets

**B**esides the planets, there are many smaller bodies orbiting the sun. These smaller bodies are asteroids, meteoroids, and comets.

### The Asteroid Belt

Asteroids are rocky bodies much smaller than any planet. Most asteroids are found between Mars and Jupiter in a region called the *asteroid belt*. There are also two big groups of asteroids orbiting along Jupiter's path.

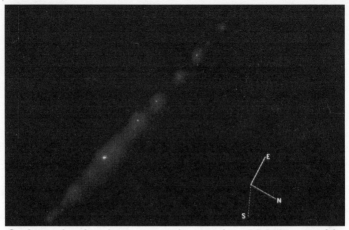

So far, scientists have named more than 22,000 asteroids. Many of these are found in the asteroid belt.

The biggest of the named asteroids is called Ceres (SAIR-eez), and it has a diameter of about 620 miles (992 km). But Ceres is unusually large. Most asteroids are much smaller.

Because they are so small, most asteroids are hard to spot. There are probably millions of asteroids floating between Mars and Jupiter. But many of these bodies may never be discovered.

The asteroids in the asteroid belt could make another planet if they stuck together. But Jupiter's gravity keeps them apart.

What happened to the dinosaurs? Scientists know that an asteroid or a comet more than 6 miles (10 km) across hit Earth about 65 million years ago. The impact threw so much dirt and water into the atmosphere that Earth's climate changed, and thousands of species of plants and animals died as a result. The dinosaurs may have become extinct during this event.

## Meteoroids

Meteoroids are rocky or metallic bodies. Like asteroids, meteoroids orbit the sun. But instead of being organized into one big band, meteoroids can be found throughout the solar system. Most meteoroids were created during collisions between two asteroids, or between an asteroid and a planet or moon.

Meteoroids sometimes enter Earth's atmosphere. When this happens, they are called meteors. Meteors get hot as they

Now I'm ready for a meteor shower.

pass through the atmosphere, and they sometimes glow brightly. If a meteor is big enough, people can see its glow as it zips across the sky. For this reason meteors are sometimes called shooting stars.

Meteors often burn up high in Earth's atmosphere. But sometimes they fall all the way to the ground. A meteor that lands on Earth's surface is called a *meteorite*.

Meteorites that are too small to be heated up by Earth's atmosphere are called *micrometeorites*.

Most meteorites are no bigger than dust specks. Every once in a while, though, a really big meteor makes its way to the ground.

## Meteor Showers

At certain points in its orbit, Earth passes through comets' leftover dust trails. Since these dust trails don't move, Earth passes through them at the exact same time each year. When this happens, lots of fiery meteors pass through Earth's atmosphere in an event called a *meteor shower.*

Here is some information about the four biggest meteor showers that occur each year:

| Name of shower | Date | Meteors per hour |
|---|---|---|
| Quadrantid | January 4 | 40–150 |
| Perseid | August 11–13 | 50–100 |
| Orionid | October 20 | 10–70 |
| Geminid | December 13 | 50–80 |

When a large meteorite hits, it leaves an impact crater that can be seen for millions or even billions of years.

The biggest meteorite on Earth weighs more than 200,000 pounds (90,720 kg)! This huge rock is in Namibia, Africa. It fell to Earth around 80,000 years ago.

The biggest meteorite on Earth is in Namibia.

## Comets

Comets are balls of dust held together by ice and frozen gases. A comet's orbit is long and oval. One end of the orbit is close to the sun. The other end is far away, in the outer reaches of the solar system.

There may be as many as 100 billion comets in the solar system.

During most of its orbit, a comet doesn't look like anything special. It is just an odd-shaped lump of matter. But when a comet gets close to the sun, something amazing starts to happen. The sun's hot rays hit the comet and melt some of its frozen matter. The melted matter gathers around the comet's "head" in a thick ball of gas and dust called a *coma*. The solar winds then blow part of the coma back from the comet in a long tail. The closer the comet gets to the sun, the longer and more spectacular its tail becomes.

Soon the comet swoops around the

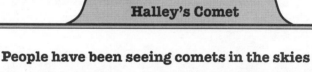

### Halley's Comet

People have been seeing comets in the skies for thousands of years. But they thought these bright streaks of light were just passing objects. Finally, in the 1700s, a scientist named Edmund Halley realized that one of these "passing objects" was actually an orbiting object that passed Earth once every 76 years. This object was named Halley's Comet in honor of its discoverer.

Halley's Comet was last visible from Earth in 1986. It will pass us again in 2062.

sun and heads back out into space. Its tail gets shorter and shorter and finally disappears. Until the comet gets close to the sun again, it will be just another tiny, hard-to-spot body zooming through the solar system.

A long time ago, in a galaxy far, far away ...

# Chapter 7
## Beyond the Solar System

**O**ur solar system is not unique. There are billions upon billions of stars just like our sun, and many of these stars have planets of their own. We can't see other planets in other solar systems — the distance is too great — but sometimes we can detect them by the effects they have on their stars. So far, scientists have found more than 60 planets outside our solar system.

It makes sense that these planets exist. The forces that created our solar system are the same everywhere, so planets have probably formed throughout the universe.

### Galaxies

Stars, their planets, and other orbiting objects do not travel through space by themselves. They are organized into groups called *galaxies* that may contain hundreds of billions of stars. Scientists estimate that our home galaxy, the Milky Way, has between 300 and 500 billion stars!

The Milky Way is a spiral galaxy,

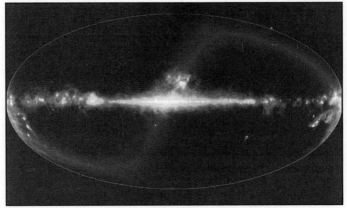

This is a picture of the Milky Way. The bright area in the middle is the center of the galaxy!

On clear, dark nights, you can sometimes see a faint white streak across the sky. This is a sideways view of a part of the Milky Way.

which means that it is shaped like a giant pinwheel. It has a thick *nucleus* (center) and many thinner arms that stretch out into space. (Our solar system is on one of the arms, about halfway out from the nucleus.)

Galaxies are so far apart that the distances can't be measured in miles and kilometers. Instead, scientists use a unit called a light-year, which stands for the

## Galaxy Guide

**There are four different types of galaxies.**

• *Spiral galaxies*, like the Milky Way, look like flat pinwheels.

• *Barred spiral galaxies* have a bright nucleus and two enormous spiral arms.

• *Elliptical galaxies* are more or less round. They are like glowing balls.

• *Irregular galaxies* can be any random shape.

Barred spiral

Elliptical

Spiral

Irregular

distance light travels in one year. One light-year is almost 6 trillion miles (9.6 trillion km). Andromeda, the closest major galaxy to the Milky Way, is more than 2 million light-

The Milky Way is part of a group of about 30 galaxies called the Local Cluster. At night, a portion of our home galaxy appears as a milky streak across the sky. That's how it got its name.

years away. That means that it takes over 2 million years for the light of Andromeda to travel to our galaxy. And there are billions of galaxies much farther away from us than Andromeda!

## Is Anybody Out There?

Does life exist on other planets? No one knows. But there are so many stars in the universe that it would not be surprising if life had evolved elsewhere. Distances in space are so huge, however, that we may never meet aliens, even if they do exist.

You can help to look for aliens! Go to *www. setiathome.ssl.berkeley. edu/download.html*. If your parents say it's okay, you can download a screen saver that analyzes radio data from space.

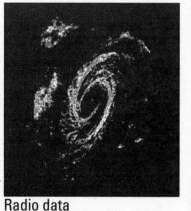

Radio data

## Birth of the Universe

The universe may have been born around 12 billion years ago in an event called the Big Bang. Before this event, all matter and energy were squeezed into a single point. But then the point

exploded, spewing gases in all directions. The gases rushed outward at incredible speeds. As they traveled, they changed into heavier forms and clumped into suns, planets, galaxies, dust clouds, and everything else that is found in space.

Humans have identified only a few thousand galaxies — a tiny fraction of all the galaxies in the universe.

Today, all of the galaxies in the universe are still moving out and away from one another. If the Big

Bang was powerful enough, this movement may continue forever. But if the Big Bang did not provide enough "push," the galaxies' gravity could slow them down someday and might even pull them back toward one another. Billions of years from now, the galaxies could come back together in an event called the Big Crunch — the exact opposite of the Big Bang.

## Back in Time

When scientists look at distant stars and galaxies, they are seeing into the past. The light from these objects has spent millions or even billions of years traveling to Earth. A scientist sees what was happening when the light first started its journey.

Imagine if your friend records a message for you on tape and then mails the tape to you. You may not get it for days, and when you listen to your friend on the tape, you'll be hearing something that happened in the past!

In the same way, light traveling from far away can tell scientists about what happened in the universe's past.

Are you ready to boldly go where no kid has gone before?

# Chapter 8
## Exploring Space

**P**eople have always been fascinated by space. For thousands of years they could only look at the skies from Earth. But in the 1950s, people learned how to launch small objects into orbit around Earth. Before long, astronauts were traveling through space in rockets. The age of space exploration had begun!

Between 1958 and 1980, more than 1,600 spacecraft were launched from Earth.

## Men on the Moon

In 1969, American astronauts Neil Armstrong, Edwin "Buzz" Aldrin, and Michael Collins traveled to the moon in a spacecraft called *Apollo 11*. Collins and the spaceship stayed in orbit while Armstrong and Aldrin flew a lunar lander down to the moon's surface.

After the lander touched down, Neil Armstrong became the first human to set foot on the moon. Millions of people watched on TV as Armstrong stepped onto the moon's rocky surface. His first words were, "That's one small step for

The first human footprint on the moon belongs to astronaut Neil Armstrong.

man, one giant leap for mankind." Armstrong and Aldrin spent more than two hours exploring the moon.

## No Weigh!

The people inside an orbiting spacecraft feel weightless. This is because they are constantly falling around Earth at the same rate as their ship. You may have experienced this sensation, called *free fall*, on a roller coaster. When the roller-coaster car is going down a very steep hill, you sometimes feel weightless for a moment. This is because you are falling toward Earth at the same rate as the roller-coaster car. This weightless feeling is neat, but it creates some problems. Everything inside a spacecraft has to be attached to something solid, like a wall or the ceiling, so it won't float around. Sleeping astronauts are strapped to their beds!

In these conditions, people can lose a lot of muscle tone. So astronauts do daily exercises to keep themselves strong and healthy.

Since *Apollo 11*'s visit, 10 more astronauts have walked on the moon. All of these people have gathered important information about Earth's closest neighbor in space.

*Apollo 11*

### Exploring the Solar System

There have been many other exciting space missions. In a very short period of time, we have learned a lot about our solar system!

In the early years of space exploration, scientists sent many spacecraft to orbit, fly past, or land on Mars and Venus. Mars probes took many incredible pictures of the Red Planet. The Venus probes did not get as many photos, but they were able to gather information about Venus's atmosphere and surface conditions. Thanks to Mars and Venus probes, we know a lot about our neighboring planets.

In 1997, a spacecraft called the Mars *Pathfinder* landed on Mars. It released a robotic vehicle called the *Sojourner* that studied Mars's rocks and soil. The *Sojourner* sent data back to Earth for almost three months before it lost power.

One especially exciting space mission was made by two spacecraft, *Voyager 1* and *Voyager 2*. Launched in 1977, both

*Voyager 1*

*Voyager 2*

vehicles flew past Jupiter and Saturn. *Voyager 2* continued on to Uranus and Neptune. The *Voyager* missions discovered many things that helped scientists to understand the outer planets — and they're not done yet. The *Voyagers* are still speeding through space, giving scientists a close-up look at the solar system.

## Turn Left at the Next Star

Steering a space vehicle is much different from driving a car or even flying a plane. To change direction, a spacecraft uses small rockets called *thrusters*.

When a thruster fires, it pushes the spacecraft in the opposite direction. If a thruster on the left front of the vehicle fires, for instance, the vehicle's nose is pushed to the right, and the spacecraft turns in that direction.

Pluto is the only planet in our solar system that has not been visited. Maybe a probe will travel to this small, cold planet someday soon.

## Watching the Skies

Scientists can also explore space from the ground. Observatories around the world contain powerful telescopes. Using these telescopes, scientists can study the sun, the planets of our solar system, other stars, and much more.

Many observatories are built on tall mountaintops. This is because Earth's atmosphere partly blocks our view into space. It's kind of like looking through a steam cloud. But the higher up a telescope is, the less atmosphere there is above it. So telescopes on mountains can get better pictures of space than lower-down telescopes can.

There are even some orbiting telescopes! Telescopes in space don't have to look through any atmosphere at all, so they can get *really* good pictures. The

The Hubble Space Telescope didn't work very well when it was first launched. Astronauts had to visit the telescope and fix it in space.

The Hubble Space Telescope is one of our most important tools for studying outer space.

Hubble Space Telescope is the most famous orbiting telescope. Launched in 1990, the Hubble Space Telescope has taken many amazing photographs of distant objects.

## Learning About Space

Today, scientists are still busy learning about space. They look at objects through telescopes. They also learn from astronauts. Several times a year, people travel into space aboard the space shuttle (a rocket-launched ship that can take off, orbit Earth, and then land again safely) and other vehicles. They orbit Earth for several days and do scientific experiments to discover new things about space.

Valeri Polyakov, a Russian astronaut — or *cosmonaut* — spent 438 days in a row on the space station *Mir*. This is the longest amount of time any human being has spent in space.

Some astronauts spend even more time in orbit. They stay in space stations for several months and figure out the best ways for people to live in space. The information they gather will be very important if humans ever try to build colonies on the moon or Mars.

The International Space Station (ISS) is being built right now! When it is finished, the ISS will be an enormous laboratory circling Earth. The first pieces of the ISS were launched into orbit in 1998. Living areas were assembled over the next couple of years. In November 2000, a crew of three astronauts moved into the ISS. They stayed for about four months. There have been more crews since then. Each crew helps to build the station.

The International Space Station should be finished in 2006. This orbiting laboratory will be the largest man-made object in outer space. Astronauts from all over the world will live there, studying the mysteries of the solar system.

It's time to get your space facts straight.

FACT OR FICTION?

# Chapter 9
## Space Myths

**M**any people have false beliefs about space. Some of these false beliefs come from books, movies, and TV shows. Others come from confusing phrases or words. However they get started, false beliefs give us wrong ideas about the solar system and the universe.

So what are some of the myths, and what are the realities?

**Myth #1:** Astronomy is the same thing as astrology.

**Fact:**

Astronomy and astrology are two very different things.

Astronomy is the scientific study of objects outside Earth's atmosphere, including stars, planets, galaxies, outer space, and more. Scientists who study these things are called astronomers.

Astrologers use symbols like these to stand for the positions and motions of the stars.

Astronomers are scientists who use tools like telescopes to study the universe.

Astrology is not a science. People called astrologers study the positions of the planets and stars and try to predict the effects these positions will have on people's lives. Astrologers' predictions are called *horoscopes*. Horoscopes are fun to read, but there is no scientific proof that they ever come true.

Hundreds of years ago, most astronomers were also astrologers. They used the scientific data they collected to make very detailed horoscopes. But eventually, astronomy and astrology grew apart. Now astronomers and astrologers are very different. They use very different tools and have very different goals. But they both love to study the motion of the stars.

Orion

Cassiopeia

For thousands of years, people have been "connecting the dots" to draw pictures in the stars. Star pictures are called *constellations*. Some constellations represent people, and others look like animals or objects.

There are 88 named constellations. Some of these constellations have been recognized for more than 6,000 years!

Lepus

Ursa Minor (the "Little Dipper")

Ursa Major (the "Big Dipper")

Leo

**Myth #2:**   Space travel is fast and easy.

Take us to super-hyper-warp speed!

**Fact:**

People travel between distant planets, stars, and galaxies all the time in science-fiction movies and TV shows.

But nobody knows how to do this in real life. The distances are too great. It would take an astronaut six months just to travel to Mars. It would take about 10 years to get to Pluto. And it would take thousands of years to travel to the nearest star!

Writers have invented things like

An astronaut could not travel to another star. The trip would take much longer than a human lifetime. But if a spacecraft were big enough to hold many families, then human beings might be able to make the trip. The astronauts who reached the new star would not be the same ones who had left Earth, however. They would be the distant descendants of the original space travelers.

"warp speed" and "hyperspace" that let their characters travel quickly between distant regions of space. But these things are just made up.

> The space shuttle orbits Earth at a speed of about 17,000 miles per hour (27,200 kph). At that speed, it can circle Earth in only an hour and a half.

Scientists haven't figured out any way to beat the space speed limit.

**Myth #3:** Planets, moons, and comets shine because they create light.

**Fact:**

Many objects shine in the night sky. Our moon is the brightest of these objects. Some planets and comets also shine. But these bodies are not creating the light that we see. They are reflecting the sun's light.

Meteors *do* create their own light as they plunge through Earth's atmosphere. They get red-hot and glow as they travel.

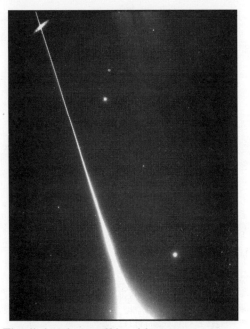

The light given off by this meteor may have been as bright as the full moon.

**Myth #4:** All of the small, shiny objects we see in our night sky are stars.

**Fact:**

Most of the twinkling lights we see in the night sky are stars. But some of them are not stars at all. A light could be a planet. It could be an approaching comet.

Or it could even be an entire galaxy, so far away that it looks like a tiny fuzzy white spot.

Sometimes you can even see satellites and spaceships passing overhead. They shine just like stars, but they move in a steady, straight path across the sky.

Only five planets — Mercury, Venus, Mars, Jupiter, and Saturn — can be seen from Earth without a telescope.

Check out *www.spaceflight.nasa. gov/realdata/sightings/index.html* to learn when the International Space Station will fly over your home.

## A Stellar Summary

In the past 100 years or so, we have learned a lot about space. Within our own solar system, we have discovered new planets and moons. Outside our solar system, we have discovered new galaxies, and we have learned that there are other planetary systems in the universe. But although we have learned a lot, there is much more to discover. With the help of telescopes and space vehicles, scientists will keep looking for new knowledge. What will they find next? No one knows. That's what makes space exploration so exciting. The sky's *not* the limit — the universe is!

# INDEX

Aldrin, Edwin "Buzz," 61, 62

Andromeda, 56–57

*Apollo 11*, 61

Armstrong, Neil, 61–62

Asteroid belt, 45–46

Asteroids, 2, 7, 46

    in dinosaurs' extinction, 47

    versus planets, 42–44

Astrology, 70–72

Astronauts, 68–69, 75

    on International Space Station, 69

    on moon, 61–63

Astronomy, 70–75

Atmosphere, Earth, 23–24

Axis, 4


Big Bang, 58–59

Big Crunch, 59


Ceres, 46

Charon, 41–42

Collins, Michael, 61

Collisions, random, 8–9

Coma, 51

Comets, 2, 7, 50

    colliding with planets, 9

    in dinosaurs' extinction, 47

    orbit of, 50–52

    versus planets, 42–44

Constellations, 73

Corona, 14

Cosmonauts, 63, 68

Craters, 8


Day, 6

Diameter, 11

Dinosaurs, death of, 47
Dust clouds, 2, 6

Earth, 2
    axis of, 4
    day on, 6
    facts about, 27
    formation of, 7
    impact craters on, 8
    life on, 23–24
    meteors in atmosphere of, 47–48
    orbit of, 3
    seen from space, 21–23
    in solar system, 1
    surface of, 23
Eclipse, 14, 15
Exploration, 60–69

Free fall, 62

Galaxies, 54–57
    distance between, 55–56
    gravity of, 59
    identified, 58
    shapes of, 55, 56
Gas clouds, 2, 7
Gas giants, 28–39
    rings of, 33
Global warming, 20
Gravitation/gravity, 6–7
    of galaxies, 59
    of sun, 10
Great Dark Spot, 37, 38
Great Red Spot, 30–31
Greenhouse effect, 20

Halley, Edmund, 51
Halley's Comet, 51, 52
Heat energy, 11
Horoscopes, 72
Hubble Space Telescope, 66–67
Hydrogen gas
    of Jupiter, 29–30
    of Saturn, 32
    of sun, 14

Impact crater, 8
International Space Station (ISS), 69

Jupiter, 2
    comets colliding with, 9
    day on, 6
    facts about, 38
    formation of, 7
    Great Red Spot on, 30–31
    hydrogen gas layer of, 29–30
    moons of, 2
    rotation speed of, 30
    size of, 28–29
    *Voyager* missions to, 65

Kuiper Belt, 40

Light
    reflection of, 76
    from sun, 11
    traveling from distant stars, 59
Light-years, 55–56

Mars, 2
    facts about, 27
    formation of, 7

    probes to, 63–64
    search for life on, 26
    surface of, 24
    weather on, 25, 26
Mercury, 2
    day on, 17
    facts about, 26
    formation of, 7
    orbit of, 3–4
    surface of, 17–18
    temperatures on, 16–17
    year of, 5
Meteor showers, 49
Meteorites
    biggest, 49, 50
    impact craters from, 49
    size of, 48–49
Meteoroids, 2, 47–48
Meteors, 47–48
    light from, 78
Micrometeorites, 48
Milky Way, 54–55
*Mir* space station, 68
Moons, 2
    exploration of, 61–63
    first human footprint on, 61
    formation of, 7
    of Pluto, 41–42
    waxing and waning of, 22
Myths, 70–78

Neptune, 2
    discovery of, 37
    facts about, 39
    formation of, 7
    Great Dark Spot on, 37, 38

Pluto in orbit of, 43
size and atmosphere of, 36–37
storms on, 37–38
*Voyager 2* mission to, 37–38, 65
Neutrons, 11
Night sky, lights in, 77–78
Nuclear fusion, 12

Observatories, 66–67
Olympus Mons, 25
Orbiting bodies, 2
Orbits, speed of, 4–5

*Pathfinder*, Mars, 64
Photosphere, 12–13
Planet X, 44
Planets, 2. *See also specific planets*
versus asteroids and comets, 42–44
axis of, 4
beyond solar system, 53–54
formation of, 6–7
on fringes, 40–44
gas giants, 28–39
inner, 16–27
life on, 57
in night sky, 78–79
orbits of, 3–4, 4–5
rotation of, 5–6
Pluto, 2, 65
facts about, 44
moon of, 41–42
orbit of, 4, 43
as planet or asteroid, 42–44
size of, 40
year of, 5
Polyakov, Valeri, 68

Protons, 11
Proxima Centauri, 10–11

Radio data, 57
Red giants, 14
Rotation, 5–6

Satellites, 22, 79
Saturn, 2
    density of, 33–34
    facts about, 39
    formation of, 7
    gassy layer of, 32–33
    moons of, 2
    rings of, 31–32, 33
    storms on, 32–33
    *Voyager* missions to, 65
Seasons, 4
*Sojourner,* 64
Solar eclipse, 14, 15
Solar flares, 13
Solar system
    birth of, 6–7
    changing, 8–9
    Earth in, 1
    edges of, 3
    exploration of, 63–65
    planets and moons in, 3–6
    size of and objects in, 2–3
    space beyond, 53–59
    stability of, 8–9
Solar winds, 11, 51
Space missions, 63–65
Space shuttle, 68, 76
Spacecraft
    launched from Earth, 60

steering of, 65
weightlessness in, 62
*Spaceflight.nasa.gov*, 78
Stars. *See also* Sun
    beyond solar system, 53
    blinking of, 33
    constellations of, 73
    distance from Earth, 10–11
    evening or morning, 19
    in night sky, 77–78
Sun, 2, 10–11
    core of, 12
    gravitational pull of, 7, 10
    life cycle of, 14–15
    photosphere of, 12–13
    size and weight of, 11–12, 13
    surface of, 13
    total eclipse of, 14, 15

Telescopes, 66–67
Thrusters, 65

Universe, birth of, 58–59
Uranus, 2
    ammonia and methane clouds of, 35–36
    day on, 35
    distance of from sun, 34
    facts about, 39
    formation of, 7
    moons of, 2
    orbit of, 37
    rotation of, 34–35
    *Voyager 2* mission to, 65

Venus, 2, 18
    conditions on, 18–20

day on, 6
facts about, 27
formation of, 7
probes to, 20–21, 63–64
temperatures on, 20
Volcanoes, of Mars, 24–25
*Voyager 1*
mission of, 64–65
pictures of Saturn's rings, 31–32
*Voyager 2*
mission of, 64–65
pictures of Neptune, 37–38

Weightlessness, 62
White dwarf, 15

Year, 4–5

Photo Credits:

Congratulations, you're a space expert! Now you're ready to join my class on their trip to outer space. It's an out-of-this-world adventure!

**Blast off with**

The **Magic School Bus**

A science **CHAPTER BOOK**

**#4**

**SPACE EXPLORERS**